The Passion Novena

A Scriptural Rosary

Larry London

Our Sunday Visitor Publishing Division
Our Sunday Visitor, Inc.
Huntington, Indiana 46750

Scripture selections in this work are taken with permission from the *New American Bible*, Copyright © 1991,
1986, 1970 by the Confraternity of Christian Doctrine,
Washington, D.C. 20017, and are used by license of
copyright owner. ALL RIGHTS RESERVED.

Library of Congress Catalog Card Number: 95-73145
ISBN: 0-87973-733-6

Illustrations by: Robert F. McGovern
Cover design by: Monica Watts
PRINTED IN THE UNITED STATES OF AMERICA
733

INTRODUCTION

With such ease can one take the wide path and drift away from Our Lord. Indeed, many are the worldly allurements that persistently tug and pull us toward those dangerous side streets along our sojourn. How easy it is to aimlessly drift with the seemingly overwhelming flow of humanity in their hustle, seldom praying or contemplating the ways of the Lord.

The narrow path that leads to Heaven seems at times to be so very hard to follow. It need not be. We often make journeying with Jesus unnecessarily difficult. In the hectic pace we set for our lives we find it oh-so-easy to not take time to read the signs along the way or enter the rest stops of the Lord.

Jesus has promised to be with us every step of life's journey. Our Mother, the Blessed Virgin Mary, will pray with us and for us as we travel life's way. The Holy Scriptures have been given to us as a light which will illuminate the narrow path to Heaven. We need not travel alone in the darkness!

What better help in our journey through the trials and tribulations of this world than to meditate upon Jesus and His Passion? With our Blessed Mother we pray and meditate on that great Passion Week that Jesus experienced with the hope that we may be strengthened and, from His example, learn how we might stay on the narrow path in times of trial.

Narrowly defined, Our Lord's Passion was from His agony in the garden until His death. The Passion's broader understanding is from Palm Sunday (Passion Sunday) until the Resurrection (Easter). It is this latter, eight-day, vision of the Passion that the *Passion Novena Scriptural Rosary* focuses upon. One additional preparation day of reflection and repentance, ideally including the Sacrament of Reconciliation, has been incorporated, thus forming a Rosary meditation of nine days — a novena of Rosaries.

Praying for an intention over the course of nine days is a practice that goes all the way back to the time of the Apostles. The "Novena of the Apostles" was those nine days between the Lord's Ascension and Pentecost when they prayed for the coming of the Holy Spirit.

The most perfect time to begin the "Passion Novena Scriptural Rosary" would be on the Saturday before Palm Sunday, with the novena's last day being Easter Sunday. The novena may, of course, be prayed at any time. There is never a wrong time to pray and meditate on that which is at the very heart of our faith, the Lord's Passion.

Praying the Scriptures with our Blessed Mother in a group setting can be especially beautiful. Each Scripture passage has been divided with a slash (/) so that it may easily be proclaimed in a two-part fashion, as is common when the Rosary is prayed by more than one person.

We humbly, but with confidence, ask our dear Mother Mary to pray with us and guide us in her loving way. Each time that we pray this novena may our hearts and minds come to more deeply understand and appreciate all that her Son, Our Lord, suffered and accomplished for us through His Passion. May we, with the Blessed Virgin's help, come to more clearly see Our Lord's way to the Father.

The Mysteries

THE PREPARATORY
MYSTERIES

O my God, please help me to see myself clearly with an understanding that will allow me to turn from the sin in my life and live in a manner pleasing to you. You alone can answer the plea of my crying heart. Only you, O Lord, *can fill that emptiness within the innermost chamber of my being. Forgive me my sins, Lord, and fill me with the joy of your salvation so that my life might have that meaning and purpose which you desire for me.*

In the name of the Father, and of the Son, and of the Holy Spirit. Amen.

First Prepatory Mystery
The Lament of Sin

✤ *Our Father* ✤

To the man he said: "Because you listened to
  your wife and ate from the tree of which I
  had forbidden you to eat, /
  "Cursed be the ground because of you!
  In toil shall you eat its yield
  all the days of your life."

Genesis 3:17

✤ *Hail Mary* ✤

When he expelled the man, he settled him east of
  the garden of Eden; /
and he stationed the cherubim and the fiery
  revolving sword, to guard the way to the
  tree of life.

Genesis 3:24

✠ *Hail Mary* ✠

Happy the man who follows not
    the counsel of the wicked/
Nor walks in the way of sinners,
    nor sits in the company of the insolent.

Psalm 1:1

✠ *Hail Mary* ✠

Not so the wicked, not so; /
    they are like chaff which the wind drives
    away.

Psalm 1:4

✠ *Hail Mary* ✠

Therefore in judgment the wicked shall not
    stand, /
    nor shall sinners, in the assembly of the just.

Psalm 1:5

✠ *Hail Mary* ✠

For the LORD watches over the way of the just, /
    but the way of the wicked vanishes.

Psalm 1:6

✠ *Hail Mary* ✠

The fool says in his heart, "There is no God." /
Such are corrupt; they do abominable deeds;
    there is not one who does good.

Psalm 14:1

✤ *Hail Mary* ✤

The LORD looks down from heaven upon the
   children of men, /
   to see if there be one who is wise and seeks
      God.

Psalm 14:2

✤ *Hail Mary* ✤

All alike have gone astray; they have become
   perverse; /
   there is not one who does good, not even one.

Psalm 14:3

✤ *Hail Mary* ✤

Oh, that out of Zion would come the salvation of
   Israel! /
   When the LORD restores the well-being of his
      people.

Psalm 14:7

✤ *Hail Mary* ✤

✤ *Glory Be* ✤

Second Prepatory Mystery
The Longing for God

✤ *Our Father* ✤

As the hind longs for the running waters, /
  so my soul longs for you, O God.

Psalm 42:2

✤ *Hail Mary* ✤

Athirst is my soul for God, the living God. /
  When shall I go and behold the face of God?

Psalm 42:3

✤ *Hail Mary* ✤

My tears are my food day and night,
  as they say to me day after day, /
"Where is your God?"

Psalm 42:4

✤ *Hail Mary* ✤

Those times I recall …
When I went with the throng
  and led them in procession to the house of
    God, /
Amid loud cries of joy and thanksgiving.…

Psalm 42:5

✤ *Hail Mary* ✤

Why are you so downcast, O my soul?
  Why do you sigh within me? Hope in God! /
For I shall again be thanking him,
  in the presence of my savior and my God.

Psalm 42:6

✤ *Hail Mary* ✤

Only in God is my soul at rest; /
from him comes my salvation.

Psalm 62:2

✤ *Hail Mary* ✤

He only is my rock and my salvation, /
My stronghold; I shall not be disturbed at all.

Psalm 62:3

✤ *Hail Mary* ✤

O God, you are my God whom I seek;
for you my flesh pines and my soul thirsts /
like the earth, parched, lifeless and without
water.

Psalm 63:2

✤ *Hail Mary* ✤

Thus have I gazed toward you in the sanctuary /
to see your power and your glory.

Psalm 63:3

✤ *Hail Mary* ✤

For your kindness is a greater good than life; /
my lips shall glorify you.

Psalm 63:4

✤ *Hail Mary* ✤

✤ *Glory Be* ✤

Third Prepatory Mystery
Promise of the Messiah

✤ *Our Father* ✤

O God, with your judgment endow the king, /
   and with your justice, the king's son.

Psalm 72:1

✤ *Hail Mary* ✤

He shall govern your people with justice /
   and your afflicted ones with judgment.

Psalm 72:2

✤ *Hail Mary* ✤

He shall defend the afflicted among the people, /
   save the children of the poor, and crush the
   oppressor.

Psalm 72:4

✤ *Hail Mary* ✤

May he endure as long as the sun, /
   and like the moon through all generations.

Psalm 72:5

✤ *Hail Mary* ✤

He shall be like rain coming down on the
   meadow, /
   like showers watering the earth.

Psalm 72:6

13

✤ *Hail Mary* ✤

Justice shall flower in his days, /
    and profound peace, till the moon be no
    more.

Psalm 72:7

✤ *Hail Mary* ✤

For he shall rescue the poor man when he cries
    out, /
    and the afflicted when he has no one to help
    him.

Psalm 72:12

✤ *Hail Mary* ✤

He shall have pity for the lowly and the poor; /
    the lives of the poor he shall save.

Psalm 72:13

✤ *Hail Mary* ✤

From fraud and violence he shall redeem them, /
    and precious shall their blood be in his sight.

Psalm 72:14

✤ *Hail Mary* ✤

May his name be blessed forever;
    as long as the sun his name shall remain. /
In him shall all the tribes of the earth be blessed.

Psalm 72:17

✤ *Hail Mary* ✤

✤ *Glory Be* ✤

Fourth Preparatory Mystery
The Call to Repentance

✤ *Our Father* ✤

In those days John the Baptist appeared, preaching in the desert of Judea saying, /
"Repent, for the kingdom of heaven is at hand!"

Matthew 3:1-2

✤ *Hail Mary* ✤

It was of him that the prophet Isaiah had spoken when he said: /
"A voice of one crying out in the desert, 'Prepare the way of the Lord, make straight his paths.' "

Matthew 3:3

✤ *Hail Mary* ✤

John wore clothing made of camel's hair and had a leather belt around his waist. /
His food was locusts and wild honey.

Matthew 3:4

✤ *Hail Mary* ✤

15

At that time Jerusalem, all Judea, and the whole region around the Jordan were going out to him /

and were being baptized by him in the Jordan River as they acknowledged their sins.

Matthew 3:5-6

✤ *Hail Mary* ✤

He said to the crowds who came out to be baptized by him, /

"You brood of vipers! Who warned you to flee from the coming wrath?"

Luke 3:7

✤ *Hail Mary* ✤

"Produce good fruits as evidence of your repentance; and do not begin to say to yourselves, 'We have Abraham as Our Father,'/

for I tell you, God can raise up children to Abraham from these stones."

Luke 3:8

✤ *Hail Mary* ✤

"Even now the ax lies at the root of the trees. /

Therefore every tree that does not produce good fruit will be cut down and thrown into the fire."

Luke 3:9

✤ *Hail Mary* ✤

And the crowds asked him, "What then should we do?" /

He said to them in reply, "Whoever has two cloaks should share with the person who has none. And whoever has food should do likewise."

Luke 3:10-11

✤ *Hail Mary* ✤

John answered them all, saying, "I am baptizing you with water, but one mightier than I is coming. I am not worthy to loosen the thongs of his sandals. /

He will baptize you with the holy Spirit and fire."

Luke 3:16

✤ *Hail Mary* ✤

"His winnowing fan is in his hand to clear his threshing floor and to gather the wheat into his barn, /

but the chaff he will burn with unquenchable fire."

Luke 3:17

✤ *Hail Mary* ✤
✤ *Glory Be* ✤

17

Fifth Preparatory Mystery
Repentance

✤ *Our Father* ✤

Have mercy on me, O God, in your goodness; /
    in the greatness of your compassion wipe out
    my offense.

Psalm 51:3

✤ *Hail Mary* ✤

Thoroughly wash me from my guilt /
    and of my sin cleanse me.

Psalm 51:4

✤ *Hail Mary* ✤

For I acknowledge my offense, /
    and my sin is before me always.

Psalm 51:5

✤ *Hail Mary* ✤

"Against you only have I sinned,
and done what is evil in your sight"— /
That you may be justified in your sentence,
    vindicated when you condemn.

Psalm 51:6

✤ *Hail Mary* ✤

There is no health in my flesh because of your
    indignation; /

18

there is no wholeness in my bones because of
    my sin.

                               Psalm 38:4

✤ *Hail Mary* ✤

For my iniquities have overwhelmed me; /
    they are like a heavy burden, beyond my
    strength.

                               Psalm 38:5

✤ *Hail Mary* ✤

Turn away your face from my sins, /
    and blot out all my guilt.

                              Psalm 51:11

✤ *Hail Mary* ✤

A clean heart create for me, O God, /
    and a steadfast spirit renew within me.

                              Psalm 51:12

✤ *Hail Mary* ✤

Cast me not out from your presence, /
    and your holy spirit take not from me.

                              Psalm 51:13

✤ *Hail Mary* ✤

Give me back the joy of your salvation, /
    and a willing spirit sustain in me.

                              Psalm 51:14

✤ *Hail Mary* ✤

✤ *Glory Be* ✤

THE MANIFESTATION MYSTERIES

*D*ear Jesus, never allow me to become lax and take the Good News of your salvation for granted. Help me to always have a heart and mind which hold great awe, wonder, and thankfulness for the marvelous works you *have wrought. Who would have believed that the Lord of Creation would take on human flesh so that we might become free of sin's grasp? With all my heart I thank you, my Lord, for revealing yourself to me. May all come to know you.*

Come, Lord Jesus, come. Amen.

First Manifestation Mystery
The Ministry Begins

✣ *Our Father* ✣

After John had been arrested, Jesus came to Galilee /

proclaiming the gospel of God.

Mark 1:14

✣ *Hail Mary* ✣

He left Nazareth and went to live in Capernaum by the sea, /

in the region of Zebulun and Naphtali.

Matthew 4:13

✣ *Hail Mary* ✣

That what had been said through Isaiah the prophet might be fulfilled... /

"the people who sit in darkness have seen a great light."

Matthew 4:14,16

22

✤ *Hail Mary* ✤

"On those dwelling in a land overshadowed by
    death /
light has arisen."

Matthew 4:16

✤ *Hail Mary* ✤

From that time on, Jesus began to preach and
    say, /
"Repent, for the kingdom of heaven is at hand."

Matthew 4:17

✤ *Hail Mary* ✤

He went around all of Galilee, /
teaching in their synagogues.

Matthew 4:23

✤ *Hail Mary* ✤

Proclaiming the gospel of the kingdom, /
and curing every disease and illness among the
    people.

Matthew 4:23

✤ *Hail Mary* ✤

His fame spread to all of Syria, and they brought
    to him all who were sick /
with various diseases and racked with pain.

Matthew 4:24

✤ *Hail Mary* ✤

Those who were possessed, lunatics, and paralytics, /
and he cured them.

Matthew 4:24

✤ *Hail Mary* ✤

And great crowds from Galilee, the Decapolis, Jerusalem, and Judea, /
and from beyond the Jordan followed him.

Matthew 4:25

✤ *Hail Mary* ✤

✤ *Glory Be* ✤

Second Manifestation Mystery
The Rejection at Nazareth

✤ *Our Father* ✤

He came to Nazareth, where he had grown up, /
and went according to his custom into the synagogue on the sabbath day.

Luke 4:16

✤ *Hail Mary* ✤

He stood up to read and was handed a scroll of

the prophet Isaiah. /

He unrolled the scroll and found the passage where it was written...

Luke 4:16-17

❧ *Hail Mary* ❧

"The Spirit of the Lord is upon me, because he has anointed me to bring glad tidings to the poor. /

He has sent me to proclaim liberty to captives and recovery of sight to the blind, to let the oppressed go free.

Luke 4:18

❧ *Hail Mary* ❧

Rolling up the scroll, he handed it back to the attendant and sat down, /

and the eyes of all in the synagogue looked intently at him.

Luke 4:20

❧ *Hail Mary* ❧

He said to them, "Today this scripture passage / is fulfilled in your hearing."

Luke 4:21

❧ *Hail Mary* ❧

And all spoke highly of him and were amazed at the gracious words that came from his

mouth. /
They also asked, "Isn't this the son of Joseph?"

Luke 4:22

✤ *Hail Mary* ✤

He said to them, "Surely you will quote me this
proverb, 'Physician, cure yourself,' and say, /
'Do here in your native place the things that we
heard were done in Capernaum.' "

Luke 4:23

✤ *Hail Mary* ✤

And he said, "Amen, I say to you, /
no prophet is accepted in his own native place."

Luke 4:24

✤ *Hail Mary* ✤

When the people in the synagogue heard this,
they were all filled with fury. /
They rose up, and drove him out of the town.

Luke 4:28-29

✤ *Hail Mary* ✤

And led him to the brow of the hill on which
their town had been built, to hurl him down
headlong. /
But he passed through the midst of them and
went away.

Luke 4:29-30

✤ *Hail Mary* ✤

✤ *Glory Be* ✤

Third Manifestation Mystery
Call of the Fishermen

✤ *Our Father* ✤

While the crowd was pressing in on Jesus and
listening to the word of God.../
He saw two boats there alongside the lake.

Luke 5:1-2

✤ *Hail Mary* ✤

Getting into one of the boats, the one belonging
to Simon, he asked him to put out a short
distance from the shore. /
Then he sat down and taught the crowds from
the boat.

Luke 5:3

✤ *Hail Mary* ✤

After he had finished speaking, he said to
Simon, /
"Put out into deep water and lower your nets for
a catch."

Luke 5:4

✤ *Hail Mary* ✤

27

Simon said in reply, "Master, we have worked hard all night and have caught nothing, /
but at your command I will lower the nets."

Luke 5:5

✠ *Hail Mary* ✠

When they had done this, they caught a great number of fish /
and their nets were tearing.

Luke 5:6

✠ *Hail Mary* ✠

They signaled to their partners in the other boat to come to help them. /
They came and filled both boats so that they were in danger of sinking.

Luke 5:7

✠ *Hail Mary* ✠

When Simon Peter saw this, he fell at the knees of Jesus and said, /
"Depart from me, Lord, for I am a sinful man."

Luke 5:8

✠ *Hail Mary* ✠

For astonishment at the catch of fish they had made /
seized him and all those with him.

Luke 5:9

✤ *Hail Mary* ✤

Jesus said to Simon, "Do not be afraid; /
from now on you will be catching men."

Luke 5:10

✤ *Hail Mary* ✤

When they brought their boats to the shore, /
they left everything and followed him.

Luke 5:11

✤ *Hail Mary* ✤

✤ *Glory Be* ✤

Fourth Manifestation Mystery
The Feast of Tabernacles

✤ *Our Father* ✤

After this, Jesus moved about within Galilee; /
but he did not wish to travel in Judea, because
the Jews were trying to kill him.

John 7:1

✤ *Hail Mary* ✤

But the Jewish feast of Tabernacles was near. /
…he himself also went up, not openly but [as it
were] in secret.

John 7:2,10

✤ *Hail Mary* ✤

When the feast was already half over, /
Jesus went up into the temple area and began to teach.

John 7:14

✤ *Hail Mary* ✤

The Jews were amazed and said, /
"How does he know scripture without having studied?"

John 7:15

✤ *Hail Mary* ✤

Jesus answered them and said, "My teaching is not my own /
but is from the one who sent me."

John 7:16

✤ *Hail Mary* ✤

"Whoever chooses to do his will shall know /
whether my teaching if from God or whether I speak on my own."

John 7:17

✤ *Hail Mary* ✤

"Whoever speaks on his own seeks his own glory, /

but whoever seeks the glory of the one who sent him is truthful, and there is no wrong in him."

John 7:18

✤ *Hail Mary* ✤

"Stop judging by appearances, /
but judge justly."

John 7:24

✤ *Hail Mary* ✤

So they tried to arrest him, but no one laid a hand upon him /
because his hour had not yet come.

John 7:30

✤ *Hail Mary* ✤

But many of the crowd began to believe in him, and said, /
"When the Messiah comes, will he perform more signs than this man has done?"

John 7:31

✤ *Hail Mary* ✤

✤ *Glory Be* ✤

Fifth Manifestation Mystery
The Entry into Jerusalem

✣ *Our Father* ✣

As he drew near to Bethphage and Bethany at
the place called the Mount of Olives, /
he sent two of his disciples.

Luke 19:29

✣ *Hail Mary* ✣

He said, "Go into the village opposite you, and
as you enter it you will find a colt tethered
on which no one has ever sat. /
Untie it and bring it here."

Luke 19:30

✣ *Hail Mary* ✣

So they brought the colt to Jesus and put their
cloaks over it. /
And he sat on it.

Mark 11:7

✣ *Hail Mary* ✣

Many people spread their cloaks on the road, /
and others spread leafy branches that they had
cut from the fields.

Mark 11:8

✣ *Hail Mary* ✣

Those preceding him as well as those following
kept crying out: /
"Hosanna! Blessed is he who comes in the name
of the Lord!"

Mark 11:9

✤ *Hail Mary* ✤

"Blessed is the kingdom of Our Father David
that is to come! /
Hosanna in the highest!"

Mark 11:10

✤ *Hail Mary* ✤

Some of the Pharisees in the crowd said to him, /
"Teacher, rebuke your disciples."

Luke 19:39

✤ *Hail Mary* ✤

He said in reply, /
"I tell you, if they keep silent, the stones will cry
out."

Luke 19:40

✤ *Hail Mary* ✤

And when he entered Jerusalem the whole city
was shaken and asked, /
"Who is this?"

Matthew 21:10

✤ *Hail Mary* ✤

33

And the crowds replied, /
"This is Jesus the prophet, from Nazareth in
    Galilee."

Matthew 21:11

        ✤ *Hail Mary* ✤

        ✤ *Glory Be* ✤

THE KNOWING MYSTERIES

Jesus, my Lord and my God, let me never forget who you are. Being both True God and True Man, you are beyond the capability of my present understanding and yet you are a constant reminder to me of God's great love for me. Through you the world was created and *remains in existence, but still in your great love you became as one of us and endured all the pain that the world could offer you so that through you mankind might be redeemed and enter God's kingdom.*

All glory and praise to you both now and forever. Amen.

First Knowing Mystery
The Anointing at Bethany

✤ *Our Father* ✤

Six days before Passover Jesus came to Bethany, /
where Lazarus was, whom Jesus had raised from the dead.

John 12:1

✤ *Hail Mary* ✤

They gave a dinner for him there, and Martha served, /
while Lazarus was one of those reclining at table with him.

John 12:2

✤ *Hail Mary* ✤

Mary took a liter of costly perfumed oil made

from genuine aromatic nard /
and anointed the feet of Jesus and dried them
with her hair.

John 12:3

✤ *Hail Mary* ✤

Then Judas the Iscariot, one [of] his disciples,
and the one who would betray him,
said, /
"Why was this oil not sold for three hundred
days' wages and given to the poor?"

John 12:4-5

✤ *Hail Mary* ✤

He said this not because he cared about the poor
but because he was a thief /
and held the money bag and used to steal the
contributions.

John 12:6

✤ *Hail Mary* ✤

So Jesus said, "Leave her alone. /
Let her keep this for the day of my burial."

John 12:7

✤ *Hail Mary* ✤

"You always have the poor with you, /
but you do not always have me."

John 12:8

✤ *Hail Mary* ✤

"We have to do the works of the one who sent
   me while it is day. /
Night is coming when no one can work."

John 9:4

✤ *Hail Mary* ✤

"While I am in the word, /
I am the light of the world."

John 9:5

✤ *Hail Mary* ✤

"There is no salvation through anyone else, /
nor is there any other name under heaven given
   to the human race by which we are to be
   saved."

Acts 4:12

✤ *Hail Mary* ✤

✤ *Glory Be* ✤

Second Knowing Mystery
The Word

✤ *Our Father* ✤

In the beginning was the Word, and the Word
   was with God, /

and the Word was God.

John 1:1

✤ *Hail Mary* ✤

He was in the beginning with God. /
All things came to be through him, and without
    him nothing came to be.

John 1:2-3

✤ *Hail Mary* ✤

What came to be through him was life, /
and this life was the light of the human race.

John 1:3-4

✤ *Hail Mary* ✤

The light shines in the darkness, /
and the darkness has not overcome it.

John 1:5

✤ *Hail Mary* ✤

He was in the world, and the world came to be
    through him, /
but the world did not know him.

John 1:10

✤ *Hail Mary* ✤

He came to what was his own, /
but his own people did not accept him.

John 1:11

✠ *Hail Mary* ✠

But to those who did accept him he gave power
   to become children of God, /
to those who believe in his name.

John 1:12

✠ *Hail Mary* ✠

Who were born not by natural generation nor by
   human choice /
nor by a man's decision but of God.

John 1:13

✠ *Hail Mary* ✠

And the Word became flesh and made his
   dwelling among us, and we saw his glory, /
the glory as of the Father's only Son, full of
   grace and truth.

John 1:14

✠ *Hail Mary* ✠

No one has ever seen God. /
The only Son, God, who is at the Father's side,
   has revealed him.

John 1:18

✠ *Hail Mary* ✠

✠ *Glory Be* ✠

Third Knowing Mystery
The Creator

✤ *Our Father* ✤

In times past, God spoke in partial and various
ways /
to our ancestors through the prophets.

Hebrews 1:1

✤ *Hail Mary* ✤

In these last days, he spoke to us through a son, /
whom he made heir of all things and through
whom he created the universe.

Hebrews 1:2

✤ *Hail Mary* ✤

Who is the refulgence of his glory, the very
imprint of his being, /
and who sustains all things by his mighty word.

Hebrews 1:3

✤ *Hail Mary* ✤

When he had accomplished purification from
sins, /
he took his seat at the right hand of the Majesty
on high.

Hebrews 1:3

✤ *Hail Mary* ✤

He is the image of the invisible God, /
the firstborn of all creation.

Colossians 1:15

✤ *Hail Mary* ✤

For in him were created all things in heaven and
on earth, /
the visible and the invisible.

Colossians 1:16

✤ *Hail Mary* ✤

Whether thrones or dominions or principalities
or powers; /
all things were created through him and for him.

Colossians 1:16

✤ *Hail Mary* ✤

He is before all things, /
and in him all things hold together.

Colossians 1:17

✤ *Hail Mary* ✤

He is the head of the body, the church. /
He is the beginning, the firstborn from the dead,
that in all things he himself might be
preeminent.

Colossians 1:18

✤ *Hail Mary* ✤

For in him all the fullness /
was pleased to dwell,

Colossians 1:19

✤ *Hail Mary* ✤

✤ *Glory Be* ✤

Fourth Knowing Mystery
The "I AM"

✤ *Our Father* ✤

"But," said Moses to God, "when I go to the
Israelites and say to them, 'The God of our
Fathers has sent me to you,' /
if they ask me, 'What is his name?' what am I to
tell them?"

Exodus 3:13

✤ *Hail Mary* ✤

God replied, "I am who am." Then he added, /
"This is what you shall tell the Israelites: I AM
sent me to you."

Exodus 3:14

✤ *Hail Mary* ✤

So they said to him, "Where is our Father?"
Jesus answered, /

43

"You know neither me nor my Father. If you knew me, you would know my Father also."

John 8:19

✤ *Hail Mary* ✤

He said to them, "You belong to what is below, I belong to what is above. /
You belong to this world, but I do not belong to this world."

John 8:23

✤ *Hail Mary* ✤

"That is why I told you that you will die in your sins. /
For if you do not believe that I AM, you will die in your sins."

John 8:24

✤ *Hail Mary* ✤

So Jesus said [to them], "When you lift up the Son of Man, then you will realize that I AM, /
and that I do nothing on my own, but I say only what the Father taught me."

John 8:28

✤ *Hail Mary* ✤

Abraham our Father rejoiced to see my day; /
he saw it and was glad.

John 8:56

✤ *Hail Mary* ✤

So the Jews said to him, "You are not yet fifty
  years old /
and you have seen Abraham?"

John 8:57

✤ *Hail Mary* ✤

Jesus said to them, "Amen, amen, I say to you, /
before Abraham came to be, I AM."

John 8:58

✤ *Hail Mary* ✤

So they picked up stones to throw at him; /
but Jesus hid and went out of the temple area.

John 8:59

✤ *Hail Mary* ✤

✤ *Glory Be* ✤

Fifth Knowing Mystery
Cleansing of the Temple

✤ *Our Father* ✤

Jesus entered the temple area /
and drove out all those engaged in selling and
  buying there.

Matthew 21:12

✤ *Hail Mary* ✤

He overturned the tables of the money changers /
and the seats of those who were selling doves.

Matthew 21:12

✤ *Hail Mary* ✤

And he said to them, "It is written: 'My house
shall be a house of prayer,' /
but you are making it a den of thieves."

Matthew 21:13

✤ *Hail Mary* ✤

The blind and the lame approached him in the
temple area, /
and he cured them.

Matthew 21:14

✤ *Hail Mary* ✤

When the chief priests and the scribes saw the
wondrous things he was doing, /
and the children crying out in the temple area,
"Hosanna to the Son of David," they were
indignant…

Matthew 21:15

✤ *Hail Mary* ✤

And said to him, "Do you hear what they are
saying?" Jesus said to them, /
"Yes; and have you never read the text, 'Out of

the mouths of infants and nurslings you have brought forth praise?' "

Matthew 21:16

✤ *Hail Mary* ✤

Jesus cried out and said, "Whoever believes in me believes not only in me /
but also in the one who sent me…"

John 12:44

✤ *Hail Mary* ✤

"And whoever sees me sees /
the one who sent me."

John 12:45

✤ *Hail Mary* ✤

And every day he was teaching in the temple area. /
The chief priests, the scribes, and the leaders of the people, meanwhile, were seeking to put him to death.

Luke 19:47

✤ *Hail Mary* ✤

But they could find no way to accomplish their purpose /
because all the people were hanging on his words.

Luke 19:48

❧ *Hail Mary* ❧

❧ *Glory Be* ❧

THE LOVING MYSTERIES

M y God, I love you, show me how to
love you more. Guide me along right
paths that I may never betray you and the love
that you have shown me. Help me to understand
that love is not something which I should wait
for, but rather it is a decision which I must make.

Let me not forget to look to you and your Word to find the meaning of love and not to what the world tells me that love should be. Be near and strengthen me that I may some day love as you have loved me.

In the name of the Father, and of the Son, and of the Holy Spirit. Amen.

First Loving Mystery
Love Betrayed

✤ *Our Father* ✤

… Jesus was deeply troubled and testified, /
"Amen, amen, I say to you, one of you will
betray me."

John 13:21

✤ *Hail Mary* ✤

The disciples looked at one another, /
at a loss as to whom he meant.

John 13:22

✤ *Hail Mary* ✤

One of his disciples, the one whom Jesus loved,
was reclining at Jesus' side. /

So Simon Peter nodded to him to find out whom
    he meant.

John 13:23-24

✤ *Hail Mary* ✤

He leaned back against Jesus' chest and said to
    him, /
"Master, who is it?"

John 13:25

✤ *Hail Mary* ✤

Jesus answered, "It is the one to whom I hand
    the morsel after I have dipped it." /
So he dipped the morsel and [took it and] handed
    it to Judas, son of Simon the Iscariot.

John 13:26

✤ *Hail Mary* ✤

After he took the morsel, Satan entered him. /
So Jesus said to him, "What you are going to do,
    do quickly."

John 13:27

✤ *Hail Mary* ✤

When he had left, Jesus said, "Now is the Son of
    Man glorified, /
and God is glorified in him."

John 13:31

✤ *Hail Mary* ✤

51

"My children, I will be with you only a little
    while longer. /
You will look for me, and as I told the Jews,
    'Where I go you cannot come.' "

John 13:33

✠ *Hail Mary* ✠

"I give you a new commandment: love one
    another. /
As I have loved you, so you also should love one
    another."

John 13:34

✠ *Hail Mary* ✠

"This is how all will know that you are my
    disciples, /
if you have love for one another."

John 13:35

✠ *Hail Mary* ✠

✠ *Glory Be* ✠

Second Loving Mystery
Loving God

✠ *Our Father* ✠

"Everyone who acknowledges me before others
    I will acknowledge before my heavenly
    Father. /

But whoever denies me before others, I will
deny before my heavenly Father."

Matthew 10:32-33

✤ *Hail Mary* ✤

"Whoever loves father or mother more than me
is not worthy of me, /

and whoever loves son or daughter more than
me is not worthy of me."

Matthew 10:37

✤ *Hail Mary* ✤

"And whoever does not take up his cross and
follow after me /

is not worthy of me."

Matthew 10:38

✤ *Hail Mary* ✤

"Whoever finds his life will lose it, /

and whoever loses his life for my sake will find
it."

Matthew 10:39

✤ *Hail Mary* ✤

"Whoever has my commandments and observes
them /

is the one who loves me."

John 14:21

✤ *Hail Mary* ✤

"And whoever loves me will be loved by my
  Father, /
and I will love him and reveal myself to him."

John 14:21

✤ *Hail Mary* ✤

See what love the Father has bestowed on us that
  we may be called the children of God. Yet
  so we are. /
The reason the world does not know us is that it
  did not know him.

1 John 3:1

✤ *Hail Mary* ✤

Do not love the world or the things of the world. /
If anyone loves the world, the love of the Father
  is not in him.

1 John 2:15

✤ *Hail Mary* ✤

For all that is in the world, sensual lust,
  enticement for the eyes, and a pretentious
  life, /
is not from the Father but is from the world.

1 John 2:16

✤ *Hail Mary* ✤

Yet the world and its enticement are passing
  away. /

54

But whoever does the will of God remains
forever.

1 John 2:17

✤ *Hail Mary* ✤

✤ *Glory Be* ✤

Third Loving Mystery
The Greatest Commandment

✤ *Our Father* ✤

One of the scribes … asked him, /
"Which is the first of all the commandments?"

Mark 12:28

✤ *Hail Mary* ✤

Jesus replied, "The first is this: /
'Hear, O Israel! The Lord our God is Lord
alone!' "

Mark 12:29

✤ *Hail Mary* ✤

" 'You shall love the Lord your God with all
your heart, with all your soul, /
with all your mind, and with all your strength.' "

Mark 12:30

✤ *Hail Mary* ✤

"The second is this: 'You shall love your
    neighbor as yourself.' /
There is no other commandment greater than
    these."

Mark 12:31

✤ *Hail Mary* ✤

The scribe said to him, "Well said, teacher. You
    are right is saying, /
'He is One and there is no other than he.' "

Mark 12:32

✤ *Hail Mary* ✤

"And 'to love him with all your heart, with all your
    understanding, with all your strength, /
and to love your neighbor as yourself' is worth
    more than all burnt offerings and sacrifices."

Mark 12:33

✤ *Hail Mary* ✤

And when Jesus saw that [he] answered with
    understanding, he said to him, /
"You are not far from the kingdom of God."

Mark 12:34

✤ *Hail Mary* ✤

And no one dared /
to ask him any more questions.

Mark 12:34

✤ *Hail Mary* ✤

Children, let us love not in word or speech /
but in deed and truth.

1 John 3:18

✤ *Hail Mary* ✤

And we are in the one who is true, in his Son
Jesus Christ. /
He is the true God and eternal life.

1 John 5:20

✤ *Hail Mary* ✤

✤ *Glory Be* ✤

Fourth Loving Mystery
True Love

✤ *Our Father* ✤

If I speak in human and angelic tongues but do
not have love, /
I am a resounding gong or a clashing cymbal.

1 Corinthians 13:1

✤ *Hail Mary* ✤

And if I have the gift of prophecy and
comprehend all mysteries and all knowledge;/

57

if I have all faith so as to move mountains, but do
    not have love, I am nothing.

                    1 Corinthians 13:2

✤ *Hail Mary* ✤

If I give away everything I own, and if I hand my
    body over so that I may boast /
but do not have love, I gain nothing.

                    1 Corinthians 13:3

✤ *Hail Mary* ✤

Love is patient, love is kind. It is not jealous, /
[love] is not pompous, it is not inflated.

                    1 Corinthians 13:4

✤ *Hail Mary* ✤

It is not rude, it does not seek its own interests, /
it is not quick-tempered, it does not brood over
    injury.

                    1 Corinthians 13:5

✤ *Hail Mary* ✤

It does not rejoice over wrongdoing /
but rejoices with the truth.

                    1 Corinthians 13:6

✤ *Hail Mary* ✤

It bears all things, believes all things, /
hopes all things, endures all things.

                    1 Corinthians 13:7

✤ *Hail Mary* ✤

Love never fails. If there are prophecies, they
    will be brought to nothing; /

if tongues, they will cease; if knowledge, it will
    be brought to nothing.

1 Corinthians 13:8

✤ *Hail Mary* ✤

For we know partially and we prophesy
    partially, /

but when the perfect comes, the partial will pass
    away.

1 Corinthians 13:9-10

✤ *Hail Mary* ✤

So faith, hope, love remain, these three; /
but the greatest of these is love.

1 Corinthians 13:13

✤ *Hail Mary* ✤

✤ *Glory Be* ✤

Fifth Loving Mystery
The Christian Life

✤ *Our Father* ✤

Beloved, let us love one another, because love is
    of God; /

everyone who loves is begotten by God and
knows God.

1 John 4:7

✤ *Hail Mary* ✤

Whoever is without love does not know God, /
for God is love.

1 John 4:8

✤ *Hail Mary* ✤

In this way the love of God was revealed to us: /
God sent his only Son into the world so that we
might have life through him.

1 John 4:9

✤ *Hail Mary* ✤

In this is love: not that we have loved God, /
but that he loved us and sent his Son as expiation
for our sins.

1 John 4:10

✤ *Hail Mary* ✤

Beloved, if God so loved us, /
we also must love one another.

1 John 4:11

✤ *Hail Mary* ✤

No one has ever seen God. Yet, if we love one
another, God remains in us, /

and his love is brought to perfection in us.

1 John 4:12

✤ *Hail Mary* ✤

There is no fear in love, but perfect love drives our fear /
because fear has to do with punishment, and so one who fears is not yet perfect in love.

1 John 4:18

✤ *Hail Mary* ✤

We love /
because he first loved us.

1 John 4:19

✤ *Hail Mary* ✤

If anyone says, "I love God," but hates his brother, he is a liar; /
for whoever does not love a brother whom he has seen cannot love God whom he has not seen.

1 John 4:20

✤ *Hail Mary* ✤

This is the commandment we have from him: /
whoever loves God must also love his brother.

1 John 4:21

✤ *Hail Mary* ✤

✤ *Glory Be* ✤

THE SERVING MYSTERIES

Help me to always remember, my God, that I cannot serve you without also serving others. Strengthen me that I might follow your loving example of service and forgive me, Lord, for the times when I fall short in my *attempts, for I know that there is much room for improvement in my life. I want to please you, Jesus. You alone are the Holy One; you alone are the Lord. I will fix my eyes upon you and your example as I strive to do your will.*

In the name of the Father, and of the Son, and of the Holy Spirit. Amen.

First Serving Mystery
Jesus Washes the Disciples' Feet

✤ *Our Father* ✤

Before the feast of Passover, Jesus knew that his hour had come to pass from this world to the Father. /

He loved his own in the world and he loved them to the end.

John 13:1

✤ *Hail Mary* ✤

He rose from supper and took off his outer garments. /

He took a towel and tied it around his waist.

John 13:4

✤ *Hail Mary* ✤

Then he poured water into a basin and began to wash the disciples' feet /

and dry them with the towel around his waist.

John 13:5

✤ *Hail Mary* ✤

He came to Simon Peter, who said to him, /
"Master, are you going to wash my feet?"

John 13:6

✤ *Hail Mary* ✤

Jesus answered and said to him, "What I am
doing, you do not understand now, /
but you will understand later."

John 13:7

✤ *Hail Mary* ✤

Peter said to him, "You will never wash my
feet." Jesus answered him, /
"Unless I wash you, you will have no
inheritance with me."

John 13:8

✤ *Hail Mary* ✤

Simon Peter said to him, "Master, then not only
my feet, /
but my hands and head as well."

John 13:9

✤ *Hail Mary* ✤

So when he had washed their feet [and] put his

garments back on and reclined at table again, he said to them, /

"Do you realize what I have done for you?"

John 13:12

✠ *Hail Mary* ✠

"You call me 'teacher' and 'master,' and rightly so, / for indeed I am."

John 13:13

✠ *Hail Mary* ✠

"If I, therefore, the master and teacher, have washed your feet, /

you ought to wash one another's feet."

John 13:14

✠ *Hail Mary* ✠

✠ *Glory Be* ✠

Second Serving Mystery
Having the Attitude of Jesus

✠ *Our Father* ✠

Do nothing out of selfishness or out of vainglory; /

rather, humbly regard others as more important than yourselves.

Philippians 2:3

✠ *Hail Mary* ✠

Each looking out not for his own interests, /
but [also] everyone for those of others.

Philippians 2:4

✠ *Hail Mary* ✠

Have among yourselves the same attitude /
that is also yours in Christ Jesus.

Philippians 2:5

✠ *Hail Mary* ✠

Who, though he was in the form of God, /
did not regard equality with God something to
be grasped.

Philippians 2:6

✠ *Hail Mary* ✠

Rather, he emptied himself, taking the form of a
slave, /
coming in human likeness; and found human in
appearance.

Philippians 2:7

✠ *Hail Mary* ✠

He humbled himself, becoming obedient to
death, /
even death on a cross.

Philippians 2:8

✤ *Hail Mary* ✤

So then, my beloved, obedient as you have
always been … /
work out your salvation with fear and trembling.

Philippians 2:12

✤ *Hail Mary* ✤

For God is the one who, for his good purpose, /
works in you both to desire and to work.

Philippians 2:13

✤ *Hail Mary* ✤

Do everything without grumbling or question-
ing, /
that you may be blameless and innocent.

Philippians 2:14-15

✤ *Hail Mary* ✤

Children of God without blemish in the midst of
a crooked and perverse generation, /
among whom you shine like lights in the world.

Philippians 2:15

✤ *Hail Mary* ✤

✤ *Glory Be* ✤

Third Serving Mystery
The Faithful Servant

✤ *Our Father* ✤

"Gird your loins and light your lamps and be like
    servants who await their master's return
    from a wedding, /
ready to open immediately when he comes and
    knocks."

Luke 12:35-36

✤ *Hail Mary* ✤

"Blessed are those servants whom the master
    finds vigilant on his arrival. /
Amen, I say to you, he will gird himself, have
    them recline at table, and proceed to wait
    on them."

Luke 12:37

✤ *Hail Mary* ✤

"Be sure of this: if the master of the house had
    known the hour when the thief was coming, /
he would not have let his house be broken into."

Luke 12:39

✤ *Hail Mary* ✤

"You also must be prepared, for at an hour you
    do not expect, /

68

the Son of Man will come."

Luke 12:40

✠ *Hail Mary* ✠

Then Peter said, "Lord, is this parable /
meant for us or for everyone?"

Luke 12:41

✠ *Hail Mary* ✠

And the Lord replied, "Who then, is the faithful
and prudent steward /
whom the master will put in charge of his
servants to distribute [the] food allowance
at the proper time?"

Luke 12:42

✠ *Hail Mary* ✠

"Blessed is that servant /
whom his master on arrival finds doing so."

Luke 12:43

✠ *Hail Mary* ✠

"Truly, I say to you, /
he will put him in charge of all his property."

Luke 12:44

✠ *Hail Mary* ✠

"That servant who knew his master's will but
did not make preparations /

nor act in accord with his will shall be beaten
    severely;"

Luke 12:47

✤ Hail Mary ✤

"… much will be required of the person
    entrusted with much, /
and still more will be demanded of the person
    entrusted with more."

Luke 12:48

✤ Hail Mary ✤

✤ Glory Be ✤

Fourth Serving Mystery
The True Disciple

✤ Our Father ✤

"Not everyone who says to me, 'Lord, Lord,'
    will enter the kingdom of heaven, /
but only the one who does the will of my Father
    in heaven."

Matthew 7:21

✤ Hail Mary ✤

"Many will say to me on that day, /
'Lord, Lord, did we not prophesy in your name?' "

Matthew 7:22

70

✤ *Hail Mary* ✤

" 'Did we not drive out demons in your name? /
Did we not do mighty deeds in your name?' "

Matthew 7:22

✤ *Hail Mary* ✤

"Then I will declare to them solemnly, 'I never
    knew you. /
Depart from me, you evildoers.' "

Matthew 7:23

✤ *Hail Mary* ✤

"Everyone who listens to these words of mine
    and acts on them /
will be like a wise man who built his house on
    rock."

Matthew 7:24

✤ *Hail Mary* ✤

"The rain fell, the floods came, and the winds
    blew and buffeted the house. /
But it did not collapse; it had been set solidly on
    rock."

Matthew 7:25

✤ *Hail Mary* ✤

"And everyone who listens to these words of
    mine but does not act on them /

71

will be like a fool who built his house on
sand."

Matthew 7:26

✤ *Hail Mary* ✤

"The rain fell, the floods came, and the winds
blew and buffeted the house. /
And it collapsed and was completely ruined."

Matthew 7:27

✤ *Hail Mary* ✤

When Jesus finished these words, /
the crowds were astonished at his teaching.

Matthew 7:28

✤ *Hail Mary* ✤

For he taught them as one having authority, /
and not as their scribes.

Matthew 7:29

✤ *Hail Mary* ✤

✤ *Glory Be* ✤

Fifth Serving Mystery
The Children of Light

✤ *Our Father* ✤

So be imitators of God, /
as beloved children.

Ephesians 5:1

✤ *Hail Mary* ✤

And live in love, as Christ loved us and handed
himself over for us /
as a sacrificial offering to God for a fragrant
aroma.

Ephesians 5:2

✤ *Hail Mary* ✤

Immorality or any impurity or greed must not
even be mentioned among you, /
as is fitting among holy ones.

Ephesians 5:3

✤ *Hail Mary* ✤

No obscenity or silly or suggestive talk, /
which is out of place, but instead, thanksgiving.

Ephesians 5:4

✤ *Hail Mary* ✤

Let no one deceive you with empty arguments, /

for because of these things the wrath of God is
coming upon the disobedient.

Ephesians 5:6

✤ *Hail Mary* ✤

So do not be associated with them. /
For you were once darkness, but now you are
light in the Lord.

Ephesians 5:7-8

✤ *Hail Mary* ✤

Live as children of light, /
for light produces every kind of goodness and
righteousness and truth.

Ephesians 5:8-9

✤ *Hail Mary* ✤

Take no part in the fruitless works of darkness;
rather expose them, /
for it is shameful even to mention the things
done by them in secret.

Ephesians 5:11-12

✤ *Hail Mary* ✤

Watch carefully then how you live, not as
foolish persons but as wise, /
making the most of every opportunity, because
the days are evil.

Ephesians 5:15-16

⚜ *Hail Mary* ⚜

Therefore, do not continue in ignorance, /
but try to understand what is the will of the Lord.

Ephesians 5:17

⚜ *Hail Mary* ⚜

⚜ *Glory Be* ⚜

THE LAST SUPPER
MYSTERIES

M y Lord Jesus, words cannot explain
nor could the human mind comprehend
the depths of what you initiated at that Last
Supper. Then and now you offer the most
wonderful nourishment possible, yourself. To

partake in your life, in your very being, is more than man can understand or even dream possible. Help me to always seek, in truth through you, the oneness that you desire with all who are called by your name so that the world may come to believe in you.

Blessed be Jesus, forever. Amen.

First Last Supper Mystery **The Eucharist**

✤ *Our Father* ✤

When the day of the Feast of Unleavened Bread arrived /
the day for sacrificing the Passover lamb.

Luke 22:7

✤ *Hail Mary* ✤

He sent out Peter and John, instructing them, /
"Go and make preparations for us to eat the Passover."

Luke 22:8

✤ *Hail Mary* ✤

They asked him, /
"Where do you want us to make the preparations?"

Luke 22:9

✤ *Hail Mary* ✤

And he answered them, "When you go into the city, a man will meet you carrying a jar of water. /

Follow him into the house that he enters."

Luke 22:10

✤ *Hail Mary* ✤

"He will show you a large upper room that is furnished. /

Make the preparations there."

Luke 22:12

✤ *Hail Mary* ✤

Then they went off and found everything exactly as he had told them, /

and there they prepared the Passover.

Luke 22:13

✤ *Hail Mary* ✤

While they were eating, Jesus took bread, said the blessing, broke it, /

and giving it to his disciples said, "Take and eat; this is my body."

Matthew 26:26

✤ *Hail Mary* ✤

Then he took a cup, gave thinks, and gave it to them, saying, /

"Drink from it, all of you."

Matthew 26:27

✤ *Hail Mary* ✤

"For this is my blood of the covenant, /
which will be shed on behalf of many for the
forgiveness of sins."

Matthew 26:28

✤ *Hail Mary* ✤

"I tell you, from now on I shall not drink this
fruit of the vine until the day /
when I drink it with you new in the kingdom of
my Father."

Matthew 26:29

✤ *Hail Mary* ✤

✤ *Glory Be* ✤

Second Last Supper Mystery
Discourse on the Father

✤ *Our Father* ✤

Philip said to him, "Master, show us the Father, /
and that will be enough for us."

John 14:8

✤ *Hail Mary* ✤

Jesus said to him, "Have I been with you for so long
a time and you still do not know me, Philip? /
Whoever has seen me has seen the Father. How
can you say, 'Show us the Father?' "

John 14:9

✤ *Hail Mary* ✤

"Do you not believe that I am in the Father and
the Father is in me? The words that I speak
to you I do not speak on my own. /
The Father who dwells in me is doing his works."

John 14:10

✤ *Hail Mary* ✤

"Believe me that I am in the Father and the
Father is in me, /
or else, believe because of the works
themselves."

John 14:11

✤ *Hail Mary* ✤

"Amen, amen, I say to you, whoever believes in
me will do the works that I do, /
and will do greater ones than these, because I am
going to the Father."

John 14:12

✤ *Hail Mary* ✤

"And whatever you ask in my name, I will do, /

so that the Father may be glorified in the Son."

John 14:13

✤ *Hail Mary* ✤

"If you ask anything of me in my name, /
I will do it."

John 14:14

✤ *Hail Mary* ✤

"In a little while the world will no longer see me, /
but you will see me, because I live and you will
live."

John 14:19

✤ *Hail Mary* ✤

"On that day you will realize that I am in my
Father /
and you are in me and I in you."

John 14:20

✤ *Hail Mary* ✤

"Whoever has my commandments and observes
them is the one who loves me. /
And whoever loves me will be loved by my
Father, and I will love him and reveal
myself to him."

John 14:21

✤ *Hail Mary* ✤
✤ *Glory Be* ✤

81

Third Last Supper Mystery
The World's Hatred

✤ *Our Father* ✤

"If the world hates you, /
realize that it hated me first."

John 15:18

✤ *Hail Mary* ✤

"If you belonged to the world, the world would
love its own; /
but because you do not belong to the world …
the world hates you."

John 15:19

✤ *Hail Mary* ✤

" '… No slave is greater than his master.' /
If they persecuted me, they will also persecute
you."

John 15:20

✤ *Hail Mary* ✤

"And they will do all these things to you on
account of my name, /
because they do not know the one who sent me."

John 15:21

✤ *Hail Mary* ✤

"If I had not come and spoken to them, they

would have no sin; /
but as it is they have no excuse for their sin."

John 15:22

✤ *Hail Mary* ✤

"Whoever hates me /
also hates my Father."

John 15:23

✤ *Hail Mary* ✤

"If I had not done works among them that no one
else ever did, they would not have sin; /
but as it is, they have seen and hated both me and
my Father."

John 15:24

✤ *Hail Mary* ✤

"But in order that the word written in their law
might be fulfilled, /
'They hated me without cause.' "

John 15:25

✤ *Hail Mary* ✤

"When the Advocate comes whom I will send
you from the Father, /
the Spirit of truth that proceeds from the Father,
he will testify to me."

John 15:26

✤ *Hail Mary* ✤

"And you also testify, /
because you have been with me from the
beginning."

John 15:27

✤ *Hail Mary* ✤

✤ *Glory Be* ✤

Fourth Last Supper Mystery
The Departure of Jesus

✤ *Our Father* ✤

"But now I am going to the one who sent me, and
not one of you asks me, /
'Where are you going?' "

John 16:5

✤ *Hail Mary* ✤

"But I tell you the truth, it is better for you that I go. /
For if I do not go, the Advocate will not come to
you."

John 16:7

✤ *Hail Mary* ✤

"And when he comes he will convict the world /
in regard to sin and righteousness and
condemnation."

John 16:8

✣ *Hail Mary* ✣

"I have much more to tell you, /
but you cannot bear it now."

John 16:12

✣ *Hail Mary* ✣

"But when he comes, the Spirit of truth, /
he will guide you to all truth."

John 16:13

✣ *Hail Mary* ✣

"He will not speak on his own, but he will speak
what he hears, /
and will declare to you the things that are
coming."

John 16:13

✣ *Hail Mary* ✣

"He will glorify me, because he will take from
what is mine /
and declare it to you."

John 16:14

✣ *Hail Mary* ✣

"Everything that the Father has is mine; /
for this reason I told you that he will take from
what is mine and declare it to you."

John 16:15

✤ *Hail Mary* ✤

"For the Father himself loves you, because you
    have loved me /
and have come to believe that I came from God."

John 16:27

✤ *Hail Mary* ✤

"I came from the Father and have come into the
    world. /
Now I am leaving the world and going back to
    the Father."

John 16:28

✤ *Hail Mary* ✤

✤ *Glory Be* ✤

Fifth Last Supper Mystery
The Prayer of Jesus

✤ *Our Father* ✤

… He raised his eyes to heaven and said,
    "Father, the hour has come. /
Give glory to your son, so that your son may
    glorify you."

John 17:1

✤ *Hail Mary* ✤

"Now this is eternal life, that they should know
you, the only true God, /
and the one whom you sent, Jesus Christ."

John 17:3

✤ *Hail Mary* ✤

"Now glorify me, Father, with you, /
with the glory that I had with you before the
world began."

John 17:5

✤ *Hail Mary* ✤

"I revealed your name to those whom you gave
me out of the world. /
They belonged to you, and you gave them to me,
and they have kept your word."

John 17:6

✤ *Hail Mary* ✤

"Holy Father, keep them in your name that you
have given me, /
so that they may be one just as we are."

John 17:11

✤ *Hail Mary* ✤

"I do not ask that you take them out of the world /
but that you keep them from the evil one."

John 17:15

✤ *Hail Mary* ✤

"Consecrate them in the truth. /
Your word is truth."

John 17:17

✤ *Hail Mary* ✤

"I pray not only for them, /
but also for those who will believe in me through
their word."

John 17:20

✤ *Hail Mary* ✤

"So that they may all be one, as you, Father, are
in me and I in you, /
that they also may be in us, that the world may
believe that you sent me."

John 17:21

✤ *Hail Mary* ✤

"Father, they are your gift to me. I wish that
where I am they also may be with me, that
they may see my glory that you gave me, /
because you loved me before the foundation of
the world."

John 17:24

✤ *Hail Mary* ✤

✤ *Glory Be* ✤

THE PASSION MYSTERIES

*S*weet Jesus, you have given so very much
for me. What could I possibly do for you?
How utterly unfair indeed was the ridicule,
scorn, humiliation, and pain that you, Almighty
One, endured for me! That the Lord of Creation
would suffer and die on a cross to redeem me is

89

beyond my ability to fully understand. Since you have loved me so very much I will try my very best to love you in return. Yes, I trust in you and I will follow you.

All praise and thanksgiving to you, Lord, now and forever. Amen.

First Passion Mystery
The Garden of Gethsemane

✤ *Our Father* ✤

… Jesus went out with his disciples across the Kidron valley to where there was a garden, /
into which he and his disciples entered.

John 18:1

✤ *Hail Mary* ✤

Judas his betrayer also knew the place, /
because Jesus had often met there with his disciples.

John 18:2

✤ *Hail Mary* ✤

So Judas got a band of soldiers and guards from the chief priests and Pharisees /
and went there with lanterns, torches, and weapons.

John 18:3

✤ *Hail Mary* ✤

Jesus, knowing everything that was going to happen to him, /

went out and said to them, "Whom are you looking for?"

John 18:4

✤ *Hail Mary* ✤

They answered him, "Jesus the Nazorean." /
He said to them, "I AM."

John 18:5

✤ *Hail Mary* ✤

When he said to them, "I AM," /
they turned away and fell to the ground.

John 18:6

✤ *Hail Mary* ✤

So he again asked them, "Whom are you looking for?" /
They said, "Jesus the Nazorean."

John 18:7

✤ *Hail Mary* ✤

Jesus answered, "I told you that I AM. /
So if you are looking for me, let these men go."

John 18:8

✤ *Hail Mary* ✤

Then Simon Peter, who had a sword, drew it, /
struck the high priest's slave, and cut off his
    right ear.

John 18:10

✤ *Hail Mary* ✤

Jesus said to Peter, "Put your sword into its
    scabbard. /
Shall I not drink the cup that the Father gave
    me?"

John 18:11

✤ *Hail Mary* ✤

✤ *Glory Be* ✤

Second Passion Mystery
The Arrest and Denial

✤ *Our Father* ✤

After arresting him they led him away and took
    him into the house of the high priest; /
Peter was following at a distance.

Luke 22:54

✤ *Hail Mary* ✤

They lit a fire in the middle of the courtyard and
    sat around it, /

and Peter sat down with them.

Luke 22:55

✤ *Hail Mary* ✤

When a maid saw him seated in the light, she
    looked intently at him and said, /
"This man too was with him."

Luke 22:56

✤ *Hail Mary* ✤

But he denied it saying, /
"Woman, I do not know him."

Luke 22:57

✤ *Hail Mary* ✤

A short while later someone else saw him and
    said, "You too are one of them"; /
but Peter answered, "My friend, I am not."

Luke 22:58

✤ *Hail Mary* ✤

About an hour later, still another insisted, /
"Assuredly, this man too was with him, for he
    also is a Galilean."

Luke 22:59

✤ *Hail Mary* ✤

But Peter said, "My friend, I do not know what
    you are talking about." /

Just as he was saying this, the cock crowed, and the Lord turned and looked at Peter.

Luke 22:60-61

✤ *Hail Mary* ✤

And Peter remembered the word of the Lord … "Before the cock crows today, you will deny me three times." /
He went out and began to weep bitterly.

Luke 22:61-62

✤ *Hail Mary* ✤

The men who held Jesus in custody /
were ridiculing and beating him.

Luke 22:63

✤ *Hail Mary* ✤

They blindfolded him and questioned him, saying, /
"Prophesy! Who is it that struck you?"

Luke 22:64

✤ *Hail Mary* ✤

✤ *Glory Be* ✤

Third Passion Mystery
The Trial of Jesus

✤ *Our Father* ✤

When day came the council of elders of the
people met, both chief priests and scribes, /
and they brought him before their Sanhedrin.

Luke 22:66

✤ *Hail Mary* ✤

They said, "If you are the Messiah, tell us," but
he replied to them, /
"If I tell you, you will not believe,"

Luke 22:67

✤ *Hail Mary* ✤

They all asked, "Are you then the Son of
God?" /
He replied to them, "You say that I am."

Luke 22:70

✤ *Hail Mary* ✤

Then the whole assembly of them arose /
and brought him before Pilate.

Luke 23:1

✤ *Hail Mary* ✤

Pilate asked him, "Are you the king of the
Jews?" /

He said to him in reply, "You say so."

Luke 23:3

✤ *Hail Mary* ✤

Pilate then addressed the chief priests and the crowds, "I find this man not guilty." /

… and upon learning that he was under Herod's jurisdiction, he sent him to Herod.

Luke 23:4,7

✤ *Hail Mary* ✤

[Even] Herod and his soldiers treated him contemptuously and mocked him, /

and after clothing him in resplendent garb, he sent him back to Pilate.

Luke 23:11

✤ *Hail Mary* ✤

Pilate addressed them a third time, "What evil has this man done? /

I found him guilty of no capital crime. Therefore I shall have him flogged and then release him."

Luke 23:22

✤ *Hail Mary* ✤

With loud shouts, however, they persisted in calling for his crucifixion, /

and their voices prevailed.

Luke 23:23

✤ *Hail Mary* ✤

So he released the man who had been imprisoned for rebellion and murder, for whom they asked, /
and he handed Jesus over to them to deal with as they wished.

Luke 23:25

✤ *Hail Mary* ✤

✤ *Glory Be* ✤

Fourth Passion Mystery
The Crucifixion

✤ *Our Father* ✤

And when they came to a place called Golgotha (which means Place of the Skull), /
they gave Jesus wine to drink mixed with gall. But when he had tasted it, he refused to drink.

Matthew 27:33-34

✤ *Hail Mary* ✤

After they had crucified him, they divided his

garments by casting lots; /
then they sat down and kept watch over him
there.

Matthew 27:35-36

✤ *Hail Mary* ✤

And they placed over his head the written
charge against him: /
This is Jesus, the King of the Jews.

Matthew 27:37

✤ *Hail Mary* ✤

Standing by the cross of Jesus were his mother
and his mother's sister, /
Mary the wife of Clopas, and Mary of Magdala.

John 19:25

✤ *Hail Mary* ✤

Those passing by reviled him, shaking their heads
and saying, "You who would destroy the
temple and rebuild it in three days, /
save yourself, if you are the Son of God, [and]
come down from the cross!"

Matthew 27:39-40

✤ *Hail Mary* ✤

Likewise the chief priests with the scribes and
elders mocked him and said, /
"He saved others; he cannot save himself.... Let

him come down from the cross now, and we will believe in him."

Matthew 27:41-42

✤ *Hail Mary* ✤

"He trusted in God; let him deliver him now if he wants him. /
For he said, 'I am the Son of God.'"

Matthew 27:43

✤ *Hail Mary* ✤

And at three o'clock Jesus cried out in a loud voice, *"Eloi, Eloi, lema sabachthani?"* /
which is translated, "My God, my God, why have you forsaken me?"

Mark 15:34

✤ *Hail Mary* ✤

Jesus gave a loud cry /
and breathed his last.

Mark 15:37

✤ *Hail Mary* ✤

And behold, the veil of the sanctuary was torn in two from top to bottom. /
The earth quaked, rocks were split, tombs were opened, and the bodies of many saints who had fallen asleep were raised.

Matthew 27:51-52

✤ *Hail Mary* ✤

✤ *Glory Be* ✤

Fifth Passion Mystery
The Burial of Jesus

✤ *Our Father* ✤

Now since it was preparation day, in order that
the bodies might not remain on the cross on
the sabbath …/
the Jews asked Pilate that their legs be broken
and they be taken down.

John 19:31

✤ *Hail Mary* ✤

So the soldiers came and broke the legs of the
first and then /
of the other one who was crucified with Jesus.

John 19:32

✤ *Hail Mary* ✤

But when they came to Jesus and saw that he
was already dead, /
they did not break his legs.

John 19:33

✤ *Hail Mary* ✤

But one soldier thrust his lance into his side, /
and immediately blood and water flowed out.

John 19:34

✤ *Hail Mary* ✤

An eyewitness has testified, and his testimony is
true; /
he knows that he is speaking the truth, so that
you also may [come to] believe.

John 19:35

✤ *Hail Mary* ✤

After this, Joseph of Arimathea, secretly a
disciple of Jesus... /
came and took his body.

John 19:38

✤ *Hail Mary* ✤

Nicodemus, the one who had first come to him
at night, also came /
bringing a mixture of myrrh and aloes weighing
about one hundred pounds.

John 19:39

✤ *Hail Mary* ✤

They took the body of Jesus and bound it with
burial cloths along with the spices /
according to the Jewish burial custom.

John 19:40

✤ *Hail Mary* ✤

Now in the place where he had been crucified
there was a garden, /
and in the garden a new tomb, in which no one
had yet been buried.

John 19:41

✤ *Hail Mary* ✤

So they laid Jesus there because of the Jewish
preparation day; /
for the tomb was close by.

John 19:42

✤ *Hail Mary* ✤

✤ *Glory Be* ✤

THE PERSEVERANCE MYSTERIES

*D*ear Jesus, through my present state of trial and suffering help me to keep my eyes fixed upon you and the unfathomable joy of eternal life in your kingdom. My God, I place my trust in you. Only you can bring good out of all things which pass through my life if I but remain faithful to you. If you are for me, then who can be against me? You alone do I worship. I believe in you and I trust in you. Help me to trust you even more.

In the name of the Father, and of the Son, and of the Holy Spirit. Amen.

First Perseverance Mystery
Courage Under Persecution

✤ *Our Father* ✤

"Behold, I am sending you like sheep in the
     midst of wolves; /
so be shrewd as serpents and simple as doves."

Matthew 10:16

✤ *Hail Mary* ✤

"But beware of people, for they will hand you
     over to courts /
and scourge you in their synagogues."

Matthew 10:17

✤ *Hail Mary* ✤

"And you will be led before governors and kings
     for my sake /

as witness before them and the pagans."

Matthew 10:18

✤ *Hail Mary* ✤

"When they hand you over, do not worry about
how you are to speak or what you are to say. /
You will be given at that moment what you are
to say."

Matthew 10:19

✤ *Hail Mary* ✤

"For it will not be you who speak /
but the Spirit of your Father speaking through
you."

Matthew 10:20

✤ *Hail Mary* ✤

"Therefore do not be afraid of them. /
Nothing is concealed that will not be revealed,
nor secret that will not be known."

Matthew 10:26

✤ *Hail Mary* ✤

"And do not be afraid of those who kill the body
but cannot kill the soul; /
rather, be afraid of the one who can destroy both
soul and body in Gehenna."

Matthew 10:28

✤ *Hail Mary* ✤

"Are not two sparrows sold for a small coin? /
Yet not one of them falls to the ground without
your Father's knowledge."

Matthew 10:29

✤ *Hail Mary* ✤

"Even all the hairs of your head are counted. /
So do not be afraid; you are worth more than
many sparrows."

Matthew 10:30-31

✤ *Hail Mary* ✤

"Everyone who acknowledges me before others /
I will acknowledge before my heavenly Father."

Matthew 10:32

✤ *Hail Mary* ✤

✤ *Glory Be* ✤

Second Perseverance Mystery
Faith, Hope, and Love

✤ *Our Father* ✤

Therefore, since we have been justified by faith, /
we have peace with God through our Lord Jesus
Christ.

Romans 5:1

✤ *Hail Mary* ✤

Through whom we have gained access [by
　　faith] to this grace in which we stand, /
and we boast in hope of the glory of God.

Romans 5:2

✤ *Hail Mary* ✤

…We even boast of our afflictions, knowing
　　that affliction produces endurance, /
and endurance, proven character, and proven
　　character, hope.

Romans 5:3-4

✤ *Hail Mary* ✤

And hope does not disappoint, because the love of
　　God has been poured out into our hearts /
through the holy Spirit that has been given to us.

Romans 5:5

✤ *Hail Mary* ✤

For Christ, while we were still helpless, /
yet died at the appointed time for the ungodly.

Romans 5:6

✤ *Hail Mary* ✤

Indeed, only with difficulty does one die for a
　　just person, /
though perhaps for a good person one might
　　even find courage to die.

Romans 5:7

107

✤ *Hail Mary* ✤

But God proves his love for us in that /
while we were still sinners Christ died for us.

Romans 5:8

✤ *Hail Mary* ✤

How much more then, since we are now
justified by his blood, /
will we be saved through him from the wrath.

Romans 5:9

✤ *Hail Mary* ✤

Indeed, if, while we were enemies, we were
reconciled to God through the death of his
Son, /
how much more, once reconciled, will we be
saved by his life.

Romans 5:10

✤ *Hail Mary* ✤

Not only that, but we also boast of God through
our Lord Jesus Christ, /
through whom we have now received reconciliation.

Romans 5:11

✤ *Hail Mary* ✤

✤ *Glory Be* ✤

Third Perseverance Mystery
The Destiny of Glory

✤ *Our Father* ✤

For you did not receive a spirit of slavery to fall
    back into fear, /
but you received a spirit of adoption, through
    which we cry, *Abba*, "Father!"

                      Romans 8:15

✤ *Hail Mary* ✤

And if children, then heirs, heirs of God and
    joint heirs with Christ, /
if only we suffer with him so that we may also be
    glorified with him.

                      Romans 8:17

✤ *Hail Mary* ✤

I consider that the sufferings of this present time
    are as nothing /
compared with the glory to be revealed for us.

                      Romans 8:18

✤ *Hail Mary* ✤

For creation awaits with eager expectation /
the revelation of the children of God.

                      Romans 8:19

✣ *Hail Mary* ✣

For in hope we were saved. Now hope that sees
   for itself is not hope. /
For who hopes for what one sees?

Romans 8:24

✣ *Hail Mary* ✣

But if we hope for what we do not see, /
we wait with endurance.

Romans 8:25

✣ *Hail Mary* ✣

We know that all things work for good for those
   who love God, /
who are called according to his purpose.

Romans 8:28

✣ *Hail Mary* ✣

What then shall we say to this? /
If God is for us, who can be against us?

Romans 8:31

✣ *Hail Mary* ✣

No, in all these things we conquer over-
   whelmingly /
through him who loved us.

Romans 8:37

✣ *Hail Mary* ✣

For I am convinced that neither death, nor life,
nor angels, nor principalities, nor present
things, nor future things, nor powers, /
nor height, nor depth, nor any other creature will
be able to separate us from the love of God
in Christ Jesus our Lord.

Romans 8:38-39

✤ Hail Mary ✤

✤ Glory Be ✤

Fourth Perseverance Mystery
Running the Race

✤ Our Father ✤

… Let us rid ourselves of every burden and sin
that clings to us /
and persevere in running the race that lies before
us.

Hebrews 12:1

✤ Hail Mary ✤

While keeping our eyes fixed on Jesus, /
the leader and perfecter of faith.

Hebrews 12:2

✤ Hail Mary ✤

111

Consider how he endured such opposition from
    sinners, /

in order that you may not grow weary and lose
    heart.

Hebrews 12:3

✠ *Hail Mary* ✠

In your struggle against sin you have not yet
    resisted /

to the point of shedding blood.

Hebrews 12:4

✠ *Hail Mary* ✠

You have also forgotten the exhortation
    addressed to you as sons: /

"My son, do not disdain the discipline of the
    Lord or lose heart when reproved by him."

Hebrews 12:5

✠ *Hail Mary* ✠

"For whom the Lord loves he disciplines; /
he scourges every son he acknowledges."

Hebrews 12:6

✠ *Hail Mary* ✠

...We have had our earthly fathers to discipline
    us, and we respected them. /

Should we not [then] submit all the more to the

Father of spirits and live?

Hebrews 12:9

✤ *Hail Mary* ✤

Endure your trials as "discipline"; God treats you as sons. /

For what "son" is there whom his father does not discipline?

Hebrews 12:7

✤ *Hail Mary* ✤

At the time, all discipline seems a cause not for joy but for pain, /

yet later it brings the peaceful fruit of righteousness to those who are trained by it.

Hebrews 12:11

✤ *Hail Mary* ✤

So strengthen your drooping hands and your weak knees. /

Make straight paths for your feet, that what is lame may not be dislocated but healed.

Hebrews 12:12-13

✤ *Hail Mary* ✤

✤ *Glory Be* ✤

Fifth Perseverance Mystery
Enduring Trials

✤ *Our Father* ✤

Consider it all joy, my brothers, /
when you encounter various trials.

James 1:2

✤ *Hail Mary* ✤

For you know that testing of your faith /
produces perseverance.

James 1:3

✤ *Hail Mary* ✤

And let perseverance be perfect, so that you may
be perfect and complete, /
lacking in nothing.

James 1:4

✤ *Hail Mary* ✤

But if any of you lacks wisdom, he should ask
God /
who gives to all generously and ungrudgingly,
and he will be given it.

James 1:5

✤ *Hail Mary* ✤

Blessed is the man who perseveres in temptation,
for when he has been proved /

he will receive the crown of life that he promised to those who love him.

James 1:12

✤ *Hail Mary* ✤

No one experiencing temptation should say, "I am being tempted by God"; /
for God is not subject to temptation to evil, and he himself tempts no one.

James 1:13

✤ *Hail Mary* ✤

Rather, each person is tempted when he is lured /
and enticed by his own desire.

James 1:14

✤ *Hail Mary* ✤

Then desire conceives and brings forth sin, /
and when sin reaches maturity it gives birth to death.

James 1:15

✤ *Hail Mary* ✤

Do not be deceived my beloved brothers: all good giving and every perfect gift is from above, /
coming down from the Father of lights.

James 1:16-17

✤ *Hail Mary* ✤

He willed to give us birth by the word of truth /
that we may be a kind of firstfruits of his
    creatures.

James 1:18

✤ *Hail Mary* ✤

✤ *Glory be* ✤

THE RESURRECTION MYSTERIES

Dear Jesus, let me so fully believe and fill my life with the hope and joy of your resurrection that I may truly go out into the world and bring with power your Good News, as you commanded. Help me to always keep in *mind that my total being has a much greater calling than anything that may be achieved in this world. Help me to please you now so that through your grace I may find myself in your presence for all eternity.*

May my lips forever proclaim your glory. Amen.

First Resurrection Mystery
The Empty Tomb

✤ *Our Father* ✤

On the first day of the week, Mary of Magdala came to the tomb early in the morning, while it was still dark, /
and saw the stone removed from the tomb.

John 20:1

✤ *Hail Mary* ✤

So she ran and went to Simon Peter and to the other disciple whom Jesus loved, and told them, /
"They have taken the Lord from the tomb, and we don't know where they put him."

John 20:2

✤ *Hail Mary* ✤

So Peter and the other disciple went out /
and came to the tomb.

John 20:3

✠ *Hail Mary* ✠

They both ran, but the other disciple ran faster
than Peter /
and arrived at the tomb first.

John 20:4

✠ *Hail Mary* ✠

He bent down and saw the burial cloths there, /
but did not go in.

John 20:5

✠ *Hail Mary* ✠

When Simon Peter arrived after him, /
he went into the tomb and saw the burial cloths
there.

John 20:6

✠ *Hail Mary* ✠

And the cloth that had covered his head, not with
the burial cloths /
but rolled up in a separate place.

John 20:7

✠ *Hail Mary* ✠

Then the other disciple also went in, the one who

had arrived at the tomb first, /
and he saw and believed.

John 20:8

✤ *Hail Mary* ✤

For they did not yet understand the scripture /
that he had to rise from the dead.

John 20:9

✤ *Hail Mary* ✤

Then the disciples /
returned home.

John 20:10

✤ *Hail Mary* ✤

✤ *Glory Be* ✤

Second Resurrection Mystery
The Appearance to Mary of Magdala

✤ *Our Father* ✤

But Mary stayed outside the tomb weeping. /
And as she wept, she bent over into the tomb.

John 20:11

✤ *Hail Mary* ✤

And saw two angels in white sitting there, one at
the head /

and one at the feet where the body of Jesus had
    been.

John 20:12

✤ *Hail Mary* ✤

And they said to her, /
"Woman, why are you weeping?"

John 20:13

✤ *Hail Mary* ✤

She said to them, "They have taken my Lord, /
and I don't know where they laid him."

John 20:13

✤ *Hail Mary* ✤

When she had said this, she turned around and
    saw Jesus there, /
but did not know it was Jesus.

John 20:14

✤ *Hail Mary* ✤

Jesus said to her, "Woman, why are you
    weeping? /
Whom are you looking for?"

John 20:15

✤ *Hail Mary* ✤

She thought it was the gardener and said to him, /
"Sir, if you carried him away, tell me where you

laid him, and I will take him."

John 20:15

✤ *Hail Mary* ✤

Jesus said to her, "Mary!" /
She turned and said to him in Hebrew, "Rabbouni," which means Teacher.

John 20:16

✤ *Hail Mary* ✤

Jesus said to her, "Stop holding on to me, for I have not yet ascended to the Father. /
But go to my brothers and tell them, 'I am going to my Father and your Father, to my God and your God.' "

John 20:17

✤ *Hail Mary* ✤

Mary of Magdala went and announced to the disciples, /
"I have seen the Lord," and what he told her.

John 20:18

✤ *Hail Mary* ✤

✤ *Glory Be* ✤

Third Resurrection Mystery
Appearance to the Disciples

✤ *Our Father* ✤

On the evening of that first day of the week …
Jesus came /
and stood in their midst and said to them, "Peace
be with you."

John 20:19

✤ *Hail Mary* ✤

When he had said this, he showed them his
hands and his side. /
The disciples rejoiced when they saw the Lord.

John 20:20

✤ *Hail Mary* ✤

[Jesus] said to them again, "Peace be with you. /
As the Father has sent me, so I send you."

John 20:21

✤ *Hail Mary* ✤

And when he had said this, he breathed on them
and said to them, "Receive the holy Spirit. /
Whose sins you forgive are forgiven them, and
whose sins you retain are retained."

John 20:22-23

✤ *Hail Mary* ✤

Thomas, called Didymus, one of the Twelve, /
was not with them when Jesus came.

John 20:24

✤ *Hail Mary* ✤

So the other disciples said to him, "We have
seen the Lord." But he said to them, /
"Unless I see the mark of the nails in his hands
and put my finger into the nailmarks and
put my hand into his side, I will not
believe."

John 20:25

✤ *Hail Mary* ✤

Now a week later his disciples were again inside
and Thomas was with them. /
Jesus came, although the doors were locked,
and stood in their midst and said, "Peace be
with you."

John 20:26

✤ *Hail Mary* ✤

Then he said to Thomas, "Put your finger here
and see my hands, /
and bring your hand and put it into my side, and
do not be unbelieving, but believe."

John 20:27

✤ *Hail Mary* ✤

124

Thomas answered and said to him, /
"My Lord and my God!"

John 20:28

✤ *Hail Mary* ✤

Jesus said to him, "Have you come to believe because you have seen me? /
Blessed are those who have not seen and have believed."

John 20:29

✤ *Hail Mary* ✤

✤ *Glory Be* ✤

Fourth Resurrection Mystery
Christ the Firstfruits

✤ *Our Father* ✤

Now I am reminding you, brothers, of the gospel I preached to you, /
which you indeed received and in which you also stand.

1 Corinthians 15:1

✤ *Hail Mary* ✤

Through it you are also being saved, if you hold fast /

to the word I preached to you, unless you believed in vain.

1 Corinthians 15:2

✤ *Hail Mary* ✤

For I handed on to you as of first importance what I also received: /

that Christ died for our sins in accordance with the scriptures.

1 Corinthians 15:3

✤ *Hail Mary* ✤

That he was buried; that he was raised on the third day /

in accordance with the scriptures.

1 Corinthians 15:4

✤ *Hail Mary* ✤

That he appeared to Kephas, /

then to the Twelve.

1 Corinthians 15:5

✤ *Hail Mary* ✤

After that, he appeared to more than five hundred brothers at once, /

most of whom are still living, though some have fallen asleep.

1 Corinthians 15:6

✤ *Hail Mary* ✤

After that he appeared to James, then to all the
apostles. /

Last of all, as to one born abnormally, he
appeared to me.

1 Corinthians 15:7-8

✤ *Hail Mary* ✤

But now Christ has been raised from the dead, /
the firstfruits of those who have fallen asleep.

1 Corinthians 15:20

✤ *Hail Mary* ✤

For since death came through a human being, /
the resurrection of the dead came also through a
human being.

1 Corinthians 15:21

✤ *Hail Mary* ✤

For just as in Adam all die, so too in Christ shall
all be brought to life, /

but each one in proper order: Christ the
firstfruits; then at his coming, those who
belong to Christ.

1 Corinthians 15:22-23

✤ *Hail Mary* ✤

✤ *Glory Be* ✤

127

Fifth Resurrection Mystery
Manner of the Resurrection

✤ *Our Father* ✤

But someone may say, "How are the dead raised? /

With what kind of body will they come back?"

1 Corinthians 15:35

✤ *Hail Mary* ✤

…What you sow is not brought to life unless it dies. /

And what you sow is not the body that is to be but a bare kernel.

1 Corinthians 15:36-37

✤ *Hail Mary* ✤

There are both heavenly bodies and earthly bodies, /

but the brightness of the heavenly is one kind and that of the earthly another.

1 Corinthians 15:40

✤ *Hail Mary* ✤

So also is the resurrection of the dead. /

It is sown corruptible; it is raised incorruptible.

1 Corinthians 15:42

✤ *Hail Mary* ✤

It is sown dishonorable; it is raised glorious. /
It is sown weak; it is raised powerful.

1 Corinthians 15:43

✤ *Hail Mary* ✤

It is sown a natural body; it is raised a spiritual
body. /
If there is a natural body, there is also a spiritual
one.

1 Corinthians 15:44

✤ *Hail Mary* ✤

So, too, it is written, "The first man, Adam,
became a living being," /
the last Adam a life-giving spirit.

1 Corinthians 15:45

✤ *Hail Mary* ✤

But the spiritual was not first; /
rather the natural and then the spiritual.

1 Corinthians 15:46

✤ *Hail Mary* ✤

The first man was from the earth, earthly; /
the second man, from heaven.

1 Corinthians 15:47

✤ *Hail Mary* ✤

Just as we have born the image of the earthly
   one, /
we shall also bear the image of the heavenly
   one.

1 Corinthians 15:49

✤ *Hail Mary* ✤

✤ *Glory Be* ✤

Appendix A
Prayers of the Rosary

APOSTLES' CREED

I believe in God, the Father almighty, creator of heaven and earth; and in Jesus Christ, his only Son, our Lord; who was conceived by the Holy Spirit, born of the Virgin Mary; suffered under Pontius Pilate, was crucified, died, and was buried. He descended into hell; the third day he arose again from the dead. He ascended into heaven, and is seated at the right hand of God the Father almighty; from thence he shall come to judge the living and the dead. I believe in the Holy Spirit, the Holy Catholic Church, the Communion of Saints, the forgiveness of sins, the resurrection of the body, and life everlasting. Amen.

OUR FATHER

Our Father, who art in heaven, hallowed be thy name. Thy kingdom come. Thy will be done, on earth as it is in heaven. Give us this day our daily bread; and forgive us our trespasses as we forgive those who trespass against us; and lead us not into temptation, but deliver us from evil. Amen.

HAIL MARY

Hail Mary, full of grace, the Lord is with thee; blessed art thou among women, and blessed is the fruit of thy womb, Jesus. Holy Mary, Mother of God, pray for us sinners, now and at the hour of our death. Amen.

GLORY BE

Glory be to the Father, and to the Son, and to the Holy Spirit; as it was in the beginning, is now, and ever shall be, world without end. Amen.

FATIMA PRAYER

O my Jesus, forgive us our sins, save us from the fires of hell, and lead all souls to heaven, especially those most in need of thy mercy. *(Note: Commonly prayed after each Glory Be.)*

HAIL HOLY QUEEN

Hail, Holy Queen, Mother of mercy! Hail, our life, our sweetness, and our hope! To thee do we cry, poor banished children of Eve; to thee do we send up our sighs, mourning and weeping in this valley of tears! Turn then, most gracious advocate, thine eyes of mercy toward us; and after this, our exile, show unto us the blessed fruit of thy womb, Jesus. O clement, O loving, O sweet Virgin Mary!

(Note: It is very fitting to say the Hail Holy Queen at the end of the Rosary.)

Appendix B
How to Pray the Rosary

1. After making the Sign of the Cross, say the Apostles' Creed.

2. Say the Our Father.

3. Say three Hail Marys.

4. Say the Glory Be to the Father.

5. Announce the first mystery, then say the Our Father.

6. Read the first Scripture excerpt, then say the first Hail Mary while meditating on the mystery.

7. Repeat step 6 for the nine remaining Hail Marys in the decade.

8. Say the Glory Be to the Father.

9. Announce the second mystery, then say the Our Father. Repeat steps 6, 7 and 8 and continue with the third, fourth, and fifth mysteries in the same manner.

10. While not essential, it is very fitting to say the Hail Holy Queen at the end of the Rosary, then kiss the cross and make the Sign of the Cross.